JENNY BROWNE
New and selected poems

Other works by Jenny Browne

Texas, Being

Welcome to Freetown

Dear Stranger

The Second Reason

At Once

Glass

Jenny Browne
New and Selected Poems

TCU Press
Fort Worth, Texas

TCU Texas Poet Laureate Series

Library of Congress Control Number:2019951327

TCU Press
TCU Box 298300
Fort Worth, TX 76129
817.257.7822
www.prs.tcu.edu

To order books: 1.800.826.8911

Designed by fusion29
www.fusion29.com

contents

17

introduction

Here, in the thirteenth volume of the TCU Texas Poet Laureate Series, published by TCU Press, meet Jenny Browne of San Antonio. Jenny's life and work are a fugue of energy, compassion, and dedication.

Her exuberant poems, rich with definite cadences, deep curiosities, and multi-layered textures, voices, and personalities, feel like wake-up calls. As if they say, Here is this life I find myself in, which fascinates and confounds me. Have we paid enough attention lately? Crisscrossing energies echo the fields of voices we live among. Who are we in this company?

> I am trying to keep something alive.
> It is a slippery thing. It is re-learning
> how to breathe. It is screaming.

Jenny was born and grew up first in Indiana. She has lived or spent extended time in Alaska, West Africa, Southern France, and Mexico, and "these remain places that I return to in poems . . ." After studying Spanish in Central America, she found herself drawn to live in a place where she could hear and practice Spanish, so she accepted a one-year position doing community development and adult literacy work for the YWCA. Arriving in San Antonio on New Year's Day, 1997, the very day beloved songwriter/singer Townes Van Zandt died, she would meet her husband-to-be, native Texan photographer Scott Martin, two weeks later. They have two daughters and have now lived in old downtown San Antonio for more than twenty years.

> My Spanish words
> emerge then duck and run, so close, so far,
> confusing orange for spider, fish for sin
> and her love for free. She says she prays for me.

Jenny says, "For me, poetry begins as a conversation with the self, but I also believe in the greater conversations poetry generates." She is not afraid to talk to anyone. See her book *Dear Stranger*. A master of counterpoint and subtle weave, her radar beam of attention seems finely tuned to every moment—sometimes the poems are switchboards of care extending so many directions, beamed up to high, but always with the subtlety of idiosyncratic awareness—it's fascinating to fathom how she gets from one place to another. A startle, a dazzle of impulses enlivening the spirit . . .

> In my country orange means
> everyone should be a little more
> afraid than usual.

She's honest and funny, believing "the practice of paying close attention to the experience of being alive, and to language itself, helps us know who we are, and helps us see who others are." Living in Texas has helped prevent her from "making swooping generalizations about other people and places. Because I have learned how to look, and listen, more closely here."

> I have always slept better next to rivers

A past Michener Fellow at the University of Texas, Austin, Jenny Browne is now associate professor of English and creative writing at Trinity University in San Antonio and codirector of the Women and Gender Studies Interdisciplinary Minor. In addition, she teaches the First Year Experience course Climate Changed. She was the 2017 Texas Poet Laureate and the 2016-2018 San Antonio City Poet Laureate. In this position she focused on San Antonio's Tricentennial through "a study of the epistolary and elegiac modes of poetry and how they can communicate personal, social, and historical connections to the land, people, and cultures that make up the city's landscape in 2018."

If it's true, as Jenny says, that " . . . wisdom/begins with knowing you know nothing"—then we may feel both emptied and refreshed in these brutal seasons of human disconnection (and precious hard-won continued optimism) we are living through together. How did we get here? Why do we keep doing these strange things to one another on our spinning planet, and how do we need to change in order to survive?

> People look horrified, but do nothing.

> or

conversations involving
over-communication of some facts
under-communication of others . . .

    Jenny's care for natural ground and gravity restores sensibilities, filtering away excessive chatter and predictable thinking. Her poems create intimacy, challenge perspectives, and are unafraid of surprise. Consider her road trip series included in this book, "Until the Sea Closed Over Us and the Light Was Gone." She drove from the highest point in Texas, the Guadalupe Mountains National Park in West Texas, to the lowest point, sea level at Corpus Christi, discovering much to write and think about along the way, paring down movement to many clearer perspectives.
    Jenny Browne and I first met in person many years ago on a snowy sidewalk in Indiana. She asked me for directions. At that moment, having never even been in that town before, I was also lost. We ended up laughing and walking together, to find our destination.

Mom said *leave things*
better than you find them
especially bathrooms
and hearts.

    Since we met, Jenny Browne has been giving me directions that help me live.

Naomi Shihab Nye
San Antonio, January 2019

I

New Poems

Fellow Travelers

1.
Apache Plume

The road is a drone note
       also known as a *burden*.

I came but a short distance,
       late and thirsty, repeating

hold yourself empty,
       then *hold yourself full*.

2.
Desert Sumac

Sun rising
like an elegant
tranquilizer

considering
the hockey
stick curve

of carbon
emissions.
Considering

the hundred
year flood
again this one.

Considering
I turn red
when crushed.

3.
Creosote

That under-employed boyfriend
you could smell approaching
all summer, strumming his guitar
played only one song:
>   *I know you rider*

& so we play it again
for the ringtail, the javelina
the rattler, even
a magnificent hummingbird:
>   *gonna miss me when I'm gone.*

4.
Ocotillo

I kept thinking of the salt flats & that great Neruda line:
I want no *truck* with death.

Once I asked a man what word he would have chosen instead,
but he sped on toward Carlsbad.

Did you know *truck* comes from the old French for *barter*?

I wonder how a translator chooses between bear hug & strangle?

I didn't say let's make a deal.

Nights I still dream of the ocean, waves big enough to drown
the engine that makes them.

The exposed shoulders of the reef rise colder with the past.
Something told me

if I waited long enough I could have that back too.

GREY WOLF, GRIZZLY BEAR, WHITE-TAILED DEER

What I took to be desert bighorns
running straight up the ridge making
a sound like breaking plates didn't
turn out to be either of those things,
& what I took to be fog shoplifting
the top half of the mountain was really
something more like the problem
with trying to remember your childhood
from pictures of your childhood.
It was the blackened stump with arms
fooling me on the hillside again,
telling me to go buy a curtain
I didn't need at all, & it was the fire
you must sometimes light on purpose
& the swallow that repeated
all powerful to them was the sun,
& it was that sun still marching
up the cliff like an army that made me
wonder why the apples were smaller
this year, & so quick. We used to take
pictures of people taking pictures
& call it memory. We used to call
nostalgia an illness caused by swelling
of the brain. The painter has been trying
for days to get the color of the mountain
just right, the yellowed skirts the agave
wear in late July, other patches almost
ashen against that face. One good cloud
changes everything. The bighorn haven't
lived here for ninety years. I was thinking
this might be a way to say someone
once tried hard to water Bone Canyon
& that there are worse things than
the only pictures from your childhood
having been taken while opening gifts.

Melanoma

Pull over again & pretend to grow
as that cloudbank shouts *try me*
& tiny red spiders fall from the trees.

In the far pasture a man seeds
his own hands with smoke.
I play Bach to forget

my father's fingertips blackening
as the last morning burned.
Years in the mirror he buttoned

each day a white shirt then flexed,
fake shaking from his own strength.
From here you can almost smell

the horses getting warm.
A Palomino eating herself lame
does not pity the fallen apricots

buzzing in the Saint Augustine.
Even the wasp dragging
a wolf spider across the road

knows we need more time
to be born, smeared in our own
white grease & tar, more time

with our house on fire my god
Bach like wind suggesting
I make a rule against suggesting

what the good part of any sadness is
too soon. The story we tell ourselves
about good intentions begins

people can change but we don't
die from the truth after all.
The sun still hurts

& I make the hard sound
a car makes when it has been
all this time running.

Llano Park

Rigo keeps raking & behind him
the rattle of the gas truck
dragging its chains. I try

a quieter herb called *conejo*. Every day
walking past the coffin shop
as the light changes & every day

three boys point, looking
up until I do. The hillside behind
the house worn in dirty circles,

the kind a donkey makes
when he's tied to a stake. I thought
I told you to wait in the car,

says America, hand over our hearts.
But they were so nice out there
in the village. They were looking

down your shirt. Rigo keeps moving
the stake & the donkey stays alive.
A skin-colored lizard pulsing

on the wall, bruised behind
the eyes. I mean a me-colored
lizard. I mean the lizard-eyed men

sold single cigarettes next to a fountain
full of jacaranda blooms. Every day
at nothing. Again to hear them laugh.

MOUNTAINS BEHIND MOUNTAINS

One voice shouting *elote elote*! One saying we are not the mind
        but the thing that watches it think.

Meanwhile, my friend pins another playing card to the wall,
        one for each week of his deployment

& calls it time. Meanwhile the man I am learning
        to love better

draws himself a beard with the burnt end of a wine cork
        & calls it time. The mind

the truck that carries too much wood, brakes stinking
        on the downhill.

Darwin believed it was easier to cross the ocean than a desert.
        I have no proof, but I promise

not to cross a river deeper than my horse's chest. What horse?
        That's just a boy

pedaling by with his pot full of corn. That's just my mind,
        standing in a hole, blowing me a kiss.

BOOM

In these grassless
pastures a *hand*

the one who *pigs*
the pipeline clean.

Big Bear is a hitch
& *fish* the term for

what gets dropped
down the bore. Here,

horses of crude,
your heaven wheezes.

In the bar that boy
with Nashville teeth

sings all the money
back to sleep.

THOUGHTS ON THE PAST IN GUADALUPE COUNTY

I desired myself a gently used kayak
from a man named Skunk
& his toothless brother who explained
in great detail how yesterday's bass catch
weighed more than his common law wife.

The knots they tied to my roof rack
weaseled free before I even reached
the old state road. Was it then that
the mesquite started screaming?
For years now my friend has collected

the saddest songs he can find.
He does this instead of painting
the old gate from rust back to black,
or penning the bull that eats
his grandmother's parsley back

to the beginning. We all have
reasons for driving farther in the dark
than we ever intended. That spring
back on Brazos St, a woman yelled *Santiago!*
at the exact same time every single night,

& Santiago never came. Or Santiago
is the chorus of an old song
half in Spanish, half in gone.
Dear placenta we buried not quite
deep enough beneath the rose bush.

Dear good dog that swallowed
a soft piece of me whole.
Our daughter has grown a freckle
on her lip without speaking
a word of it. You can't tell

a forest fire to tie her shoes.
Dear every late night we sat too close
to the speakers & didn't hear a thing.
The wisdom teacher on the CD
I am trying to listen to for the seventh time

suggests that wisdom begins with knowing
you know nothing. This may or may not apply
to the river I just saw doubling back on itself,
sharp as a dirty trombone. Dear Skunk,
if the handle of your grandfather's ax

has been replaced twice since he last held it,
is it still your grandfather's ax?
Dear Skunk, I once read Ahkmatova
for three days & three nights
on a train, & was never the same.

UNTIL THE SEA CLOSED OVER US
AND THE LIGHT WAS GONE

-Dante, Canto XXVI

But if the truth is dreamed of toward the morning

El Paso

Although it was really last summer's song,
all this summer *Despacito* played on
as slower then I turned myself to gaze
at Juárez, but this summer everything
hurts my eyes, a dozen Thai boys tweezed from
inside the earth, the picnic table shirts
of those bold Croats, even words sprayed below
the bridge I walked back across: *Sabes el
camino?* Do I know the way? *Donde?*

Wolves change rivers. A swallowtail lingers.
It was summer all morning & all night
& soon it would always be summer so
I point us toward the far sea & mean
we approach the ocean like returning.

And going our lonely way through that dead land

Salt Flat

We approach the ocean like returning
soldiers, arms open wide, or we approach
the ocean like border patrol pickups
speeding six hundred fifty-something miles
of exposed skin. We approach the ocean like
poachers, galloping at the speed of blood.

We approach the ocean ripping open
our shirts to roar. We approach not to be *of*

God, but *in* God. Or we ghost approach with
no preposition at all, mirroring
the fat frack trucks speeding past, loaded down with
even wider temporary housing
as if the sea too was made quick & cheap,
thin walls already bubbling in the heat.

Till my prayer becomes a thousand

Van Horn

Thin walls already bubbling in the heat,
I consider the blanketed woman
feeding a host of sparrows before church.

(If by layers we mean how little we
can see inside another animal.)

You will be kind. You will try. You still
like the fortunes about basic human
decency best, even as the seams of
your map turn soft as tissue. (& if by

layers we mean dressed to walk all night long?)

& like every seed you will start confused,
searching long in the dark, & like every
seed you will crown out *holy holy holy is the Lord*
of hosts, the whole earth is full of his glory.

When memory returns to what I say

Balmorhea

Of hosts! The whole earth! Full of his glory!
would be Isaiah 6:3, more or less,
verses it took me until now to learn

I once buried, a churched child, only
to dig up today for our birds, our dirt,
cobblestones, & that bell that keeps ringing
without needing reason. I don't want to
make kindness heroic, although I do.

Once upon a horse I got turned around.
Once too by a god, then sent off to find
the donkey its tail. Also by the hands
of a man, first gently, then not so much.
Though he was no machete, nor was sex
two trucks stuck between Pecos & death.

But if near dawn the dreams we have are true

Pecos

Two trucks stuck between Pecos & death
makes for an uphill line to begin again.

By side, by side, they grind their teeth
& we shall not be moved. If then I felt

we were all just waves, that vague & that
abstract. Or there ought to be a law against

motion sickness, but we're born with it:
landscape as a list of future targets.

The Golden Cheeked Warbler didn't have time
to pack & if, as Dogen writes, we should

not view ash as *after*, and firewood
as *before*, what time is being told & told

but not listening? What would it be
to die, or stay alive, albeit fearlessly?

If it already happened it should not be too soon

Ozona

To die, or stay alive, albeit fearlessly,
my mind must stop revising that great hawk
into a killing machine. I don't mean
to sound so apocalyptic, but I
remind my students they can't put a drone
in their poem without some blood on their hands
or leave out the man scanning his screen for
heat. It's cold in Ozona, but I meet
the happiest men in the world also
heading east. *Nothing to do there but fish.*

Birds of a feather, gods of wind, I am
supposed to warm to your slow turning
blades of war. Mine, not oars. Arms grow sore
wishing our species better metaphors.

We made wings of our oars for our fool's flight

Seminole Canyon

Wishing our species better metaphors,
I consider the author of borders
& fear standing up the slumped horizon.

*The anthropocene's silent auction now
closing.* Author of brushing peach pie from
the geologist's beard. From here, we can
see smog hiding one of her children
behind her back. The other approaches
the canvas: our land turns blue, our eye black.

Each refugee takes her sky's temperature.
Author of those two white horses feeding
at the Val Verde County Line, reminding us

of nothing. It was still summer & it was
never their job to humanize the land.

Just like a little cloud sailing skyward

Del Rio

Never their job to humanize the land,
a hotwired breeze doubles the feeling.

Do I have a choice? jokes the man who owns
the only pho shop downtown when I ask
how he likes living here? On the border?
On earth? I thought this was a slow dance,
but we laugh until we cry, like people do:
jinx on me, jinx on you. Rain never did
follow the plow, but the soybean expert
now wants his overtime beer. Each of us
is to ourselves permanent. I remain
petty & confused by joy, a seed

in the hot blind earth. I must remember
what I cannot believe. I must remember.

It grieved me then and now again it grieves me

Rock Springs

What can I not believe? I must remember
that day outside Rock Springs when the green
needles on the cypress made it look so
easy to survive us. Outside my room
two boys built a fort of mud & sticks so
that a third might come stomp on it. Which one
will grow into the kind of man who climbs
a mountain to pick up ash another
left behind? Which will leave his tongues untied,

the dogstar blinking from his eyes. Tonight!
Buckets of iced Corona on special!
Even this thirsty one might begin to
feel oceanic out there. What between
the ocotillo & the tequila.

Only those flames, forever passing by

Sonora

The ocotillo & the tequila
& the way it becomes even harder to
breathe as ozone repeats *Do your job! Do
your job?* In a different land a man needed
only a goat to cross the century.

Nothing sadder than a train in the rain?
The methane flares do their job, burning all
the night. As does the eyelid, the moth &
even the mouth, testing out echoes in
this unfinished house. How is it the girls
in Juárez turned to dust? How is it I'm
still holding this stone? Nothing sadder than
sagging, frostbit cactus? It's a breeze to
be lost & not seem. Ask the lonely bees.

Beyond the world, the light beneath the moon

San Antonio

Be lost & not seem? Ask the lonely bees,
those tricked into believing more painted blue
ceiling meant more blue sky. *Sana sana*
echoes the mockingbird, our little grey songster.

She's heard the mothers try to make it better.
She's heard the father on the border howl

in his holding cage. We never learned to
love the way blossoms & almonds do.

In the history book of the newly born,
every room is a room of water. That
is where the dreamers land. In late July,
the river tried to love her own thinning

face like sleep. *Si no sanas hoy, sanarás mañana*
I would have liked to have known you before.

I stood on the bridge and leaned out from the edge

Laredo

I would have liked to have known you before,
your stars jeweling like migratory desire
in song above the old town. Someone leaves
the trains on all night. Until the river
again unlocks the grey bird's light, she sings.
On the promise of an empire of
monarchs protecting our only sky, she sings.
Thawed back into recognition, she sings
while on the muted television one
of those shows where a hidden camera films
a roofer using his nail gun to pin
a sleeping old woman's wig to her head.

People look horrified, but do nothing.
People look horrified, but do nothing.

May I not find the gift cause for remorse

Alice

People look horrified, but do nothing
to imagine the distance before steam,

before turbine? We could have made so much
better time. But why? Toward the shoreline with
exactly four grackles & the hard wind
some still call a *Norther*. Sort that makes
it rain sideways. Then comes the Horse Crippler
& the Greater Roadrunner repeating
the question. Comes caliche, cochineal
I-35 & missing our exit.

Did you forget where we live? *The work*
for which all other work is preparation?
Wake early & watch a girl leaning from land
to thank the water with both of her hands.

And turning our stern toward morning

Brownsville

To thank the water with both of her hands.
Do you know what is the way? Return us
to the body's surface without violence,
as we were & as we never were, still
approaching the ocean like we own it.

Despacito. Memorize the tune we
call air for the next time you need to breathe.

You say it was summer all night, all day,
& no one knows what to wear anymore.

Not skin, the citrus trees, nor the future.
            O one, o none, o no one, o you. Where
Let the way when no where it led?

Without the last of what summer's song?

Broke hard upon our bow from the new land

Corpus Christi

Although it was really last summer's song,
we approach the ocean like returning,
thin walls already bubbling in the heat
of hosts, the whole earth full of his glory.

Two trucks stuck between Pecos & death?
To die, or stay alive, albeit fearlessly?

Wishing our species better metaphors.
Never their job.
To humanize the land what can I not believe?
I must remember the ocotillo & the tequila!

To be lost & not seem, ask the lonely bees.

I would have liked to have known you before people
look horrified but do nothing
to thank the water with both of her hands.

II

Poems from *Dear Stranger* (2013)

texas, being

where blind catfish cruise
limestone caverns

from deeper we drink
while a man sweets tea

with his knife stirring
all the way down

border fires
making breathing a geography

mountain cedar
floating pollen fevers

bones in the road
sun-bleached

possum grin just missing
the curb where she

like all the modern girls
paused to consider

her inventory of elsewheres
because we can

drive ten hours and some
how still be here

From THE Presentation OF SELF In Everyday LIfe

We live by inference. I am, let us say, your guest. You do not know, you
cannot determine scientifically, that I will not steal your money or your
spoons . . .
　　　　　　—W. I. Thomas, *Social Behavior and Personality*, 1951

1.

The Last Halloween He Was

among us, Wynn dressed up
as a Fallopian tube, wrapped in elastic

bandage from ankle to chest,
with hands clasped together, mid-thigh

where they cradled a plastic sack full
of hard-boiled eggs,

dropping them one at a time,
hourly, as he moaned,

fertilize me for godsake would
somebody please . . . ?

The grey paper-mâché ovary took days to dry
before he duct-taped it to his head.

A sign above I-10 shouts LIFE, by
which it implies rhythm,

a heart-shaped pattern we might scan,
begins at 18 days, but doesn't advertise

when a man decides to terminate his own,
or what he might happen to be wearing.

2.

At Barton Springs

Behind her, a man removes and
refolds the pink meat of his sandwich.

By this he means sweetheart, yeah you, older than my
moustache, younger than my bunion.

How great, he tells us (again), *it used to be in Austin*.

From the free side of the depths,
the dogs and topless laugh
loudest.

The co-ed with *Night*
          opened across her chest
has freckles she wasn't born with.
Those of us who paid three bucks to sink and surface
feel a smidgen fenced in, but it's not so bad

here, watching

the downside of sunset slump red-faced against the cement wall
          like that tasered teenager on YouTube. Really
not bad at all.

3.

On Earth

          as it is in the bedroom,

conversations involving
over-communication of some
facts under-communication of
others,

and at the BBQ, drinking Shiner Bock
with the Defense Department translator,

her nose stud a spark in the porch light,
her reaching for another, saying

    sometimes you have to
remind yourself

    that this guy you're talking for, so polite, nice and all,

he once
sent a woman
her husband's head
in an ice chest.

4.

And When the Main Character Says

I forgot myself   she
does not mean bodily   rather

she has just made a
relatively unrehearsed verbal assertion   such
as

I love cucumbers,   but
they make me repeat like a Howitzer,   or

conserve energy; screw
and nurse at once,
even

dear stranger (*oh honey*)   mess up my hair
and

thumb me 'till   I hum.
According to the survey   we say
we are
happy.

A full three-quarters of us   say we are.

MEXICO

The nanny's truck is white and clean. She comes
inside without a key. Our kids won't eat
the food I leave, no peas, not even plums.
They want her spicy, her greasy brown meats.
Dulces she sneaks them when my head is turned.
I've tried to share how I'd like things done. *Mira*,
the rules we make for the best. My Spanish words
emerge then duck and run, so close, so far,
confusing orange for spider, fish for sin
and her love for free. She says she prays for me.
I pour her coffee, touch her hand. *Listen,*
let's try to understand each other. We
are sisters, equals, this game we're playing.
I've no idea what she is saying.

camping with strangers

In the slow mesquite going one strums a guitar. One has fingers.
One knows the words. One's backside stretches the stars
and stripes of her unfolded seat and sighs. One rubs a ridgeline

of blond stubble running up right thigh. One grills
        a pineapple; *You won't believe how sweet it gets.*
One muttering *I hate rabbits, I hate rabbits.*

Closer to the forest, dirty young men stretch white sheets
tight between trees. Could be a bug class from the college.
Could be Baptists and that their Devil Catcher.

Shadows of six legs, shadows of struggle.
In the beginning, one seeks similar species.
In the end, love eats the little head of love.

In the reddened embers one singes some proof
of her existence on a blackened foil packet of potatoes.
She's been distracted, following a faded trail map

drawn inside her, the old ways known by word of mouth.
The silence of the man sitting next to her like butterfly wings
being torn from their body. Hers green and smoking.

Behold the soft air of dusk, the watermelon and dust.
Behold sound of seeds spit to the dim distance.
We keep score and nothing grows.

He leaves the door open in hope of rain.
She wishes she had switched to wine.
Behold a distant singing. *There's a hole*

        in the middle of the road.
There's a road in the middle of midnight.
Sometimes she lies to him about where she's been

and where she's going but not
because it matters. Sometimes she lies next to him,

touching foreheads, trying to breathe.

In the morning he strokes the furry brown mound
of tarantula that slept beneath their tent. She grows wet
in the dew. There he goes, there he goes,

growing on her again, the one she married,
the way he tugs his swim trunks up too high, the way he watches
everything longer than necessary.

In the morning everyone uses both hands
to hold their own little cup of darkness.

The sausage dropped by the child in the tree
is left to turn
half dust, half flesh

of our flesh, that one who prefers wearing
her binoculars backwards. Here she comes, bug-eyed and stumbling
adjusting the focus, making all our mistakes momentarily

look several times smaller than they might in real life.

LOVE LETTER TO a STRANGER (STRANGER)

Tell us of a bypassed heart beating in 12C,
how the woman holds a stranger's hand
to the battery sewn in beneath her collarbone,
and says *feel this*. Tell us of the man's ear
listening across the aisle, hugging itself,
a fist long since blistered by blaze.
Outside, morning sun buckling up.
Inside, twitching bonesacks of bat, birdsong
erupting as light cracks the far jungle canopy.
Ten thousand feet below ours, a grey cat
tongues the morning's butter left out to soft.
Last night we broke open the sweet folds
around two paper fortunes. One said *variety*.
One said *caution*. The woman in 12C would hold that
her heart needs its hidden spark, but the man shows
how some live the rest of their lives with half a face
remembering its *before* expression. Who was it
that said our souls know one another
by smell, like horses?

LOVE LETTER TO A STRANGER (CHINA)

for my mother

Chinese medicine believes sadness a sign
of too much wind. On the mesa I watch
Summer Olympics bounced from Beijing
Authorities have been seeding clouds,
tamping their horizon's steady cigarette.
Handsprung girls land and gather back in
shuddering breaths. This is not
the year of the horse. She's tried
adding green to the canvas,
but she's not painting much anymore.
Grasshoppers snap along the dusty shoulder like
bad matches. China? We dig six inches
and hit red rock. They say your ears will fall off
if you keep pointing at the moon.

Love Letter to a Stranger (Kabul)

The back of the waitress's coffee arm holds
a grip-shaped bruise. I mean to write
how familiar that pink baby, pinching
hard for her Cheerios with such desperate
concentration, but I keep getting emails
from *A Skinnier You*, and I keep reading that
the combat mission has ended. Acid
thrown from the back of a motorcycle.
I mean email from *Hear Ladies Scream in Bed*.
I mean to dress more appropriately for this
late spring surge of freeze, and apologize
for my entire existence, but I keep feeling *(sorry)*
like some sad armadillo banging her head
on the future's poorly reinforced undercarriage,
foolish to think I can ever wake unafraid
for our daughters.

LOVE LETTER TO A STRANGER (BIRD)

Perched on the precipice of grocery cart, you scream

I've forgotten your name. *Starling, starling,*
sparrow or *finch*, say hello hollow bones
then wait a hundred bird years
before whistling into the canyon of a kind man's ear.

He'll talk of rooftops, skipping church, climbing
the sanctuary stones on fingertips, how
no one ever looked up.

Who's the face that found my name,
tied to a low-flying balloon, and never replied?

I live in _____. *I like* _____
Tell me _____.

Somewhere the nest woven from questions
that grew quiet by sky, choral in mind, a cluster
of speckled eggs gestating between *Texas*

and *thunderstorms*, that strangely familiar bird
still repeating: *Tell me your favorite color that isn't blue.*

LOVE LETTER TO A STRANGER (DOG)

One god escapes, smelling
for like pilgrims, and returns,
smelling of duckshit.
One coughs up wormy chunks

of his own heart. One is carried,
blind and incontinent, down
the steps, and back. I believe
they will wash her bed again.

One gets short chained to a pole
until his eyes crust and fly over.
Chase your flies, UPS, the wind
and our affections. Dream

of virgins. Eat the ham. I say
warm body pressed to thigh.
Thump in the night I say
it depends on the god.

THE MULTIPLE STATES OF MATTER

If four legs make a desk, a relationship, a donkey
and its hee-haw switch-backing our slow descent,
which way to turn first? If four in the morning
and distant lands cloud the green tea, shall we begin

with the sound of one blue parakeet, loyal to sky
inside its dented cage, and not the slow laugh
of the red-haired friend who watched with me,
drinking instant coffee outside Alamosa. I could

leave now and reach her before next darkness,
but I hear the hole cut into her skull like
a busted taillight, the sharp turns of her face
walled off from any new memory. I could become

the steady hands of the man who tossed a blanket
over the bird, conceal light, and call it night.
I could have throttled the Buddhist, earlier, halfway
through dinner, when he said, *the real problem is you*

still think you get to decide what kind of death is a good one.
He's right; that's precisely what I think.
The back of the donkey I rode down into the canyon
quaked beneath me for miles. Every time we stopped,

she faced the rock. She didn't want to see
where we were going either. This desk faces a wall
of wooden masks, gods and monsters, some
with other bodies coming out their foreheads.

The being growing inside my friend's brain is both
solid and liquid, what science class once explained
to be the multiple states of matter. They didn't tell us
that the real sound a heart makes is not a drum,

but a stubborn *lub-dub*, swollen and dumb in the throat.
The donkey I ride isn't going anywhere.

If the only difference between gods and monsters
exists in which brain they find belief, why not turn

toward another story that shouldn't be true, a pickup
backing over the head of a dog named Eggroll,
and how the wet earth beneath gulped to make room
for his brain to rest until the blind giant's joyride was over.

And the children cheered. And the mom wiped her eyes
on the back of her hand. And Eggroll stood and shook
is what keeps happening and happening next, but
five hundred miles away, in another state of matter,

the one who sits beside my friend's bed
must remind her how to swallow.
Every few minutes he asks, *do you need to swallow?*
and if she blinks he says, *okay, swallow then.*

TO Have consIDereD THe LasT
OF THe summer MacKereL

arriving with raw insides knifed from spine and re-arranged,
bite-sized, between the fish's own head and tail, all balanced
on a cloud of shaved Daikon, as symbolic of the presentation
of self implies an inner life similarly displayed for strangers

and lovers alike to choose the tender parts, touching them
to a puddle of soy sauce followed by the fibrous clumps
of ginger and slivered scallion, but to have considered this
particular mackerel as like us, and thus hopeless, forgets

how lucky it can feel to have already grown desperate
and driven fast from the new therapist's office, parking
on hot soft asphalt, walking through hot soft wind
into the Tokyo Inn and there been greeted by the stunned

guns of air conditioning and led to a low table in back,
and listen; that young couple at the next table have just
returned from their honeymoon and are eating tempura
with the girl's pale sweet parents. The whole family

will visit the planetarium after this, quietly staring up
at a preview of tomorrow's sky, a lump in the mother's
left breast mushrooming in the dark, the father's freckled
skin ticking toward metastases. And that girl, when asked

can't answer what the best part of her trip was, not
that her slender neck doesn't redden with it, but because
she hasn't yet discovered how the best parts eventually
point across the table at the worst, as the hook lip

of the big dipper points towards the north star,
one saying *you always*, the other *you never*.
Nights like these, when stars all start to look the same,
mackerel gray and slow flickering,

as an index finger hovers above the violently
spun globe, pressing down on this particular place
as one presses the fish's flesh, quiet and wondering,
just how long since we've seen the ocean.

THE CENTER FOR THE INTREPID

$50 Million Rehabilitation Center Opens on Fort Sam Houston
—San Antonio Express News, *January 2007*

Wheeled onto this jet leaving our town, another soldier
in first class, his pruned body echoing the earth beneath
going airborne, liberating itself from gravity.

Inside the cave of grey hoodie
he shivers as might ghost or cello,
if they could, in another dark war

when the baptism and birthday party band wrapped their music in
black plastic and dug deep by the Lempa river.

The song below stayed there until the air emptied of metal and fear.
Only the air never.

One of the first things learned
by a possible jury is that you cannot be a witness against yourself.

What then is a body? I raise my right hand.
I still have a right hand,

knees, skin that tries to explain its own brine and marrow.
Most grown-ups I know

walk around make-believing
they are in one piece. It's tomorrow, and my children want

that game they call, *You be the monster, I'll be the kid.*

TO THE MAN WHO STOLE THE TREES WE PLANTED
IN MEMORY OF MY BROTHER-IN-LAW WHO
KILLED HIMSELF EARLIER IN THE SPRING

May they grow tall, branches full of reddish-purple seeds that spit on
your pickup truck
        and choke in the throats of your gutters.
May they bring grackles   and more grackles.
May there be fungus. May there be allergies. May the wind shove
        a scratching to your bedroom window, disturbing that dream
where
    you float
the whole afternoon down a radiant river
with a second inner tube clutching your ice chest of cold beer,

and trading it for the one where a man stands alone in a
freshly dug hole
        and the rain grows nothing but deeper.
May the reincarnation of his dumb cat piss
        your Dallas Cowboys pillow.
May his Fleetwood Mac shiver the crusty dishes in your sink.
May your rooms be repainted with his second to last really bad choice
    of maroon.

May you be marooned, surrounded and drowning
        when the roots finally reach your pipes and break them
                                        as a man breaks
a pencil in his fist, and leaves
        not the reason.

TAKING CHILDREN TO THE CEMETERY

may require donuts and repetition.
No, you may not walk there.
No, you may not stand on that.

I know he is not here.
I know I said we were going to visit.
I know I said we were going to see.

II

Poems from *The Second Reason* (2007)

NOW, THAT IS summer

The day makes a map of disappearing, frenzied
rumor of hummingbird between
how we see and are seen.

Last night around the fire
a voice said, you know this conversation
only seems to be based in reality.

The day makes a map of disappearing
and the ants need a bridge
for carrying crumbs twice their size.

There are moments I pretend I am popcorn
swelling fourteen times my original size
and nobody ever looks surprised.

All I want is to watch an old lady's hand
reach through our fence for a fist of rosemary,
the spice of remembrance and wonder

how far must she carry it? How far
must it carry me? Now sputtering lines
of laughter arch from the neighbor's sprinkler

and pairs of shiny brown legs begin
their pedal through then back around
our street in endless circles.

Someone looks up and says, now that is summer.
Someone looks and says poor kids.
Someone says faster, faster.

THE SEASON OF MINT

1.
More honey while it's hot.

I stand for mint   teacher
of too little rain,

for sun's vengeance left in lemon   damp
          altar erected in a temple
called mouth.

Steep   steeper.

2.
I stand for any heart's majority

opinion against efficiency.

Does grief stirring itself
sweeten   sweeter.

3.
What war lives

in the barely hairs
on a man's earlobe,
          in this transparent green sip   oh pale soldier?

Enough stems to tea a small Arab nation.

When I say I have a soft
spot for them, he says
*I thought all your spots
were soft.*

4.

This year

      not enough

wind here

      to bend steam.

THE BODY BEFORE IT IS A BODY

I could lie and say that
on the day my country most
recently went to war I at least
changed my plans but

I went skiing.

My hat was orange and warm.
The snow, at times, blinding.

The other landscape is always internal.
I was finally pregnant but no matter
how hard I listened I couldn't hear

the noise of so much fallen
snow as it tumbles
from the steepest rooftops.

I don't mean the way the bulk shudders
into the earth but the instant
of release itself

as when the body before it is a body knows better
than this world.

Below my feet a father shouted at his still growing
red-faced, snow-caked child, *stop making noise
and do exactly what I tell you*.

On the mountain, the first thing you learn is how to stop.

In my country orange means
everyone should be a little more
afraid than usual.

THE CHEAP SEATS

When asked why the administration waited until after Labor Day to try to sell the American people on military action against Iraq. White House Chief of Staff Andrew Card replied, "From a marketing point of view, you don't introduce new products in August."
—Morning Edition, *Sept. 17, 2002*

Another gust brings the gunfire of falling pecans down on the tin roof in what sounds like a declaration of war in the silverware drawer. Two flies buzz the carcass of a black bean repeatedly. It's late fall but the high school is still not allowed to teach those two leaning against the fence sucking blurry purple bruises into one another's necks that there's a time, place and good reason to just say yes. Today may or may not be the day. They may or may not have good reason. Above their heads, red leaves are still attached to their branches but the arms and legs of the corn-fed tackles who sat in the last row of my high school Economics class are thudding in the dust along the broken back roads of Basra. And the boy on the corner? He can't raise his hands in the air and wave 'em like he just don't care if he wants to keep those pants up. Don't ask me. I'm wearing white linen way too late, eating maraschino cherries straight from the jar as a marching band of sugar ants surges across the countertop spelling N-E-X-T. These are the cheap seats. There's a cold sweat on the cheddar cheese, a nickel-sized hole in the window screen. The knives on the wall are lined up by size.

SAVING THE DAYLIGHT

My ninety-three-year-old neighbor stands in front of his Buick Regal wearing pale green shorts with cowboy boots. He sometimes misses places when he shaves. The open hood of the car shades the top half of his body. There are no other shadows. This is the day we say we will make the sun set one hour later. My neighbor has two roosters named Pierre and Sly. Sometimes they wake me earlier than I would like. It's nearly noon, too late for Benjamin Franklin. To the Parisians he suggested: *Every morning as soon as the sun shall rise, church bells and, if necessary, cannon shall inform the citizenry of the advent of light and awaken the sluggards and make them open their eyes to see their true interests.* Canadian poultry producer Marty Notenbomer objects: *The chickens do not adapt to the changed clock until several weeks have gone by so the first week of April and the last week of October are very frustrating for us.* Twice a year, my neighbor holds one battery cable in each hand and waits in the sun. The grease-stained cement looks stunned. The Parisians never woke before noon. This is the day that Franklin hath made. My neighbor says *tell me when it's time.* This is the way I would like to be changed, to hear *now* and wake on the dashboard, green and glowing exactly.

POETRY

Lately I've been listening to Springsteen sing *Stolen Car*, memorizing that part about the guy really hoping he gets caught so he doesn't disappear entirely. And when the lost wife in the song talks about the love letters and how reading them made her feel one hundred years old, I think about how you almost want her to say love letters and then one hundred times better. She could have said that.

Amarillo

There are at least two ways to speak the Spanish word for yellow. Locals rhyme it with can-a-hello, optimism included in the $39.99 Day's Inn double where the clerk whispers an explanation for her crying sister, *she wants to get married before she goes to jail so he won't find nobody else but I say he'll find somebody anyways and it'll feel a helluva lot better if they ain't married that's what they call making lemons outta lemonade.* Not exactly but now the sister's pissed and that's yellow too. Further south the double *ll* hooks into a yo-yo wiggling up to the surface like a fish I once caught far from these namesake miles of golden grain. Its lip held a dozen hooks with snapped curly strands of line where don't give in gave out. I'd still rather catch the last thought before any act that lands me sputtering in a yellow plastic bucket or in the case of a man from Pennsylvania on trial for poking the bakery aisle: pointer finger tunnels through hundreds of muffins, perfect thumbprints pressed firm into packs of Archway apricot-filled, three mutilated pumpernickels presented as evidence. I think of him in Amarillo as we follow a Mustang with a dented loaf of Wonder sunning on the dash and a hologram bumper sticker that glints *I Fear No Beer.* I mean how bad could it be, my last thought before the patchouli roommate again explained her urine therapy and the coward in me emptied, a full glass of *amarillo*, familiar and frightening as the kind of place you pass through as fast as it passes back through you.

A Man can STILL Dream of Cigarettes

The Spanish teacher said you'll know you've finally learned the language when the dream baby's snake face looks up and says *hola*. I dreamed the real baby came too soon. We put her back and went to the rodeo where women wearing jeans without back pockets leaned hard around barrels and the dust did rain. The parenting book tries to explain how it feels like you go to sleep in your bed and wake up in Mozambique. It could be China or Afghanistan. There are no camels in the Koran. We don't write what we know too well. We don't dream what we've already seen. Behind her tiny veined lids, the real baby's eyes gallop. Two hours old, each dewy thought a shiny fire truck parting the Red Sea bellowing new. There is no need to seed her mind like clouds above a barely contained blaze. The parenting book doesn't try to explain how it feels to be born. There is no way to say I wonder in Spanish. A sign above the road says you too arrived here through a tunnel in the darkness. It could say you can't be lost if you don't have a map. There are no camels in El Salvador but there are black birds that backflip on telephone wires. That is what some call a translation. The baby's toes curl around my finger like tender claws. Somewhere oil fields burn endlessly, their confused faces clearly visible from outer space.

THERE'S A SLOW GREEN RIVER I'VE BEEN LIVING BY

1.

If I were forced to begin in the midst of the hardest
movement it is starless and the dark
painted wood

of the kitchen floor lines my forehead as inside
a womb grinds her houseful of stones
into dust. A woman's voice

repeating *you are close. You have a whole boneyard of*
contractions behind you. She said boneyard.
She said behind me.

2.

Were the winter mornings when
my body was still only one body

and I ran past The Mug Club
and the crumbling bricks

of the Russian Orthodox Church, past
an aged German Shepherd turning

manic circles in the dirt and the purple
ceramic eagle bolted to the roof

of the high school, past Andy's
Taco House that used to be Bob's

Barbeque that used to be Praise the Lord
Fried Chicken just as every green shatter

of glass I stepped around used to be
whole and quenching

to where the river begins because

back then I could still pretend

there were beginnings and ends,
a being with boundaries.

3.

I have tried to be a good river fore-
          seeable and faithful
to the innate knowing what
          is bank, what is flow.
Above the red evening
          light skids off
the slopes of abandoned
          grain silos, rows of steel
breasts aimed skyward.
          They've been turned
into studios for sculptors,
          people who know the material
creates the form.

4.

A single cactus flat flung into loose dirt multiplies, peacocks out like
shallow rooted fireworks and works its thousand hands over the win-
dows, behind the gutters and under the fence reaching and reaching
like the pictures I've seen of refugees until it is all I can see and I hold
the heavy red fruit in my gloved palm and slice it lengthwise with the
sharpest knife then scoop the magenta pulp into a bowl and it is sun-
rise and it is open-heart surgery and it is placental, clotted and full of
black seeds and it stains my teeth.

5.

There's a photograph
tacked to the wall above

this desk. I am seven months
full, a pale and swollen moon floating
the sea at Vieques. The Marines called it
Green Beach. The locals, Punta Arenas, point
of sand, where the smallest part names the whole.
If the camera turned its back and followed the road
up into the hills it would see how even though the
soldiers haven't been gone long the green is al-
ready swallowing everything, moving over
the empty weapons caches, imagining
them into burial mounds or ripe
bellies, swelling multiple
selves, growing bigger
the closer we come

6.

And then.

I have always slept better next to rivers

and loved the low grind of coal barges, slow floating
            mountain ranges

that make the turn wide then wider.

And I have watched the spaces between
the scales of a garden snake expand

as animal moves through animal.

I have squinted at the sky
and seen the sun move through a pinhole

and birth is still not like
anything.

7.

I make another list

of all I have ever loved and twist it
into the open end of a bottle and leave it

more open.

8.

If the one thing I will never know is the only thing
I know it is green and it keeps moving.

In one version of this story the cypress tree bends down
and reties her own shoes but you know how that goes.

Everyone is still learning, pausing, reaching low
for the place where another kind of breathing takes hold

and grows wild and deeper. I'd like to tell you about it
but that would mean I'm talking again, using words

like contraction, dilate and divisible by
instead of following anything down and down.

See how the squirrels chew with their mouths open, scattering
green pecan pieces on our big ideas.

See how they stare back without blinking.

9.

I am trying to keep something alive.
It is a slippery thing. It is re-learning
how to breathe. It is screaming.

Say New
        Orleans.
Say black
        coffee.
Say the night
        watchmen all love

the three-legged dog who walks
his owner to the news stand.
And the news, who does it love?

Eyes, hands, some newborn sun
shattering its own face back
in the pattern of broken glass?

10.

Spring and our new dog leans into the screen door. Her vulva swollen
and dripping leaf shaped rusty smears on the porch steps. Soon we
will fix this but today we cannot contain her season. We cannot
change that blood is the sister of green or that despite the word sea-
son, meaning certain conditions into which a year is traditionally di-
vided, every-thing still seems to happen at once. Pass the frenzied
barking on both sides of the street.

11.

This could be the world. An air-
conditioned green room you've seen

before. Inside, a young man repeats
exactly what you want then misspells

your name on a recycled paper cup.
I dream a counter where you can

order your teeth any size you like.
See we can choose our coffee

but we can't choose our monsters.
This fall the earth turns itself

into a sway-backed animal,
all claws and fleas fox-rotting

round the damp stinking anus.
A single blind destructive eye.

On TV, circling red with
yellow rings and yellow

with red rings and
none of them our green.

12.

Note found inside a bottle:

I have seen several Septembers in search
of a new name. I have heard *do not rest*
and *do not forget*. I have asked why
all the parades are followed by women
with brooms. I have answered
pour the unhappiness out. I strap
my child to my back and walk
towards a river. It is the same river.

13.

The water under the bridge is filled with tiny
black fish, a school of commas. They clarify

that once I waited, grew larger, multiplied
and became two. I divided, stood and walked

on a river of selves. No remainder.
The fish swallow the o's we throw whole.

The wall echoes any word we shout. Even stop.
Even this hot. Impossible, the popsicle.

14.

If a root swallows the corner of the path, if green, if nothing
lasts, not even a child's name written with a sharp rock

on the buckled sidewalk then we must hide
the rock beneath a low blooming rosemary bush.

It will be our secret. You can find it again, each
morning like a mind, a surprise. Or a sky.

on labor street

In that dark hard to hear

what bark means *lonely* what
bark means *moon*.

Remember the waiting?

I remember the weather   new trees
      leaning east, a deep
dishwater sky.

Hikers know the first face
      to the forest gets
the spider web.

First face to be born gets a war   all that
      exploding light.

Do you want the short or long version?

A plastic bag expands on her branch,
the words *thank you* inked
      six times in red up the side.

Thank who? We will walk until we cannot walk.
Then we will walk again.

There is no short version.

Come on little dawn, you half
      comma hiccupping homeward.

The meadowlarks have been practicing for months.
A song that says *see-you, see-you*.

NOT an AUBaDe

Considering that it is evening
and we aren't going anywhere.

That we might spend the entire night passing
the baby with your deep set eyes and we're not sure

whose nose but surely my mother's long
narrow tongue, your brother's spun

yellowish hair, this small body cobbled
from ours, her road run with such

multiple shadows,
back and forth, back and forth.

Considering too that this is not
a special way of being afraid.

This is the end of every day
when we peer from the bushes

into the glowing kitchen of our own life
for a glimpse of when the three we have become

resembles two again for a few moments
as the lengths of our bodies touch

at the hip, the shoulder, the occasional
fingertip and you reach deeper

into the soapy water then pass me
the warm dripping plates to rinse and dry

and stack front to back or back to front
each with their own particular fit, at last this

slight rub, the almost forgotten hum
of my body rising, spreading, leaving

the windows all lingered in steam.

Today on Mars

Through the telescope I can see Venus.
In the mirror I can see

how I've become one of those
divided types

I loved as a child, books
where the astronaut's body fits

the mermaid's scaly tail
and the head of a chef nods.

Put glow-in-the-dark-stars
on the nursery's ceiling.

Put the head of the hammer above
this heart a glass house. I've become

one of those leaky souls,
hot and sweet

midnight milk beads
a blue translucent *we*.

Today on Mars, water.
Today in a dimple, the universe.

The baby smiles
but doesn't mean it yet.

I spend entire days
trying to find my face.

LULLABY

What makes two eyes close, a small body grow
so much heavier in sleep? The winter garden
        at dawn, hourglass-shaped
gourds no one remembers planting.

In the place where waiting meets morning
leaves are shaped like the vowels
        in evergreen. Fallen barbs
of memory. What's the first lie
you will tell your child besides everything
will be okay?

Forty steps from backdoor to gate. Forty verses
to the song with no words
        but *please*.

And the last lie you remember? Feel it surface
like a shard of glass lost in the heel for years,
flesh toughened where it touched.

There were four mittens and a bowl full of mush,
There was an old woman whispering *hush*.
Were there three older brothers fed to the alligators?
And the cauliflower you ate not to join them?

Give the brothers names like Rutabaga, Fontanelle
and Dublin. Live another minute on that island
        of tender, pulsing between
the shifting plates of her small skull.

And those shiny black crows
        fighting in the distance. Tell her
that's wet paint dancing.

THE CRY BONE'S CONNECTED TO THE WHY BONE

Cold front blasts a train through
the bedroom, one long roar
above late talk of distant war.

Numbers and names I don't recognize
climb, drift, pile higher.
There are exactly twenty-seven

bones beneath the skin of a hand.
There are not as many words
for snow as I was once told.

It's almost morning.
If you're not with us, you're dew.
If you're dew, you disappear.

If you're me this week you see
a baby learn she has hands,
the bilateral little declaration

of a common axis, grip and find.
Put your hand in the air if you've heard
the one about the hokey pokey man.

He may die but you can't bury him.
And if the whole self was never in?
Keep moving   keep moving

towards a voice you still recognize.
If you're not with us, you're a fist
and if you're a fist, you can't reach

that collection of wishbones
rattling on
the quietest shelf in the room.

THE SEASON WHEN SOME PEOPLE WILL SAY

you should always begin with scissors.
Rock is too obvious. Some people say
obviously. Some people say it's really
coming down. Some people say down is
the new up. Some people say the sky is full
of birds whose names I will never learn.
Some people say don't you remember me
and some people already know the answer
to a question before they ask it. Some people
ask if you know what you are having
and some people pretend they don't know
what some people mean by this and say yes,
a baby. Some people don't think this is funny.
Some people say you shouldn't drink coffee.
Some people say the cup is half asleep. Some
people say you will never sleep again.
Some people say I was just resting my eyes.
Some people say I hope it has your eyes.
Some people say I can't even see my feet anymore.
Some people say you should approach birth
with the calm of a stoplight changing color but yellow
means speed up or scared to death depending on
the some people in question and some people
say a dream of cherries means you will soon have
knots in your tongue. Some people say watch out
for red dye #3. Some people say produce like the word
for fruits and vegetables and not the verb that means
to make something. Some people keep a journal.
Some people say paper equals full moon, unmade bed,
cream but no sugar. Some people's mothers say don't think
you're the only one who ever made deals with God.
Some people say please and thank you. Some people
say you will never be the same. Some people say who
wants the same? Some people say you know
this isn't a game.

THE ODDS

When your friend says what are the chances, don't specify 10,000 to 1 for finding a four-leaf clover but 20,000,000 to 1 for becoming a saint. And when she says, on Friday it was just a little cough, don't remind her that this is Monday because it makes no difference to a bolt of lightning, 1 in 576, 000. From a yellow plastic chair in the corner of the hospital room say only that your friend's child looks good even if she doesn't look good, even if veins ghosting rivers through the pale skin, even if empty cereal bowls of hipbones. And if the wall of machines beeping, the tubes floating the child's leaky rowboat lungs and the face of your friend staring at numbers like reflections of a self she doesn't quite recognize, if none of this looks good say nothing. Because nothing anyone says will sound good either. Especially not *septic*, a word that belongs in the mouths of plumbers not mothers. And when, weeks later, your friend's husband says what lesson from this but don't be in the wrong place at the wrong time and your friend asks again how she is supposed to live after the worst thing that could possibly happen happens do not say good luck or but for the grace of God goes the question mark because you still know only what there is to know; the risk of dying from exposure is 1 in 225,107. And that what you really want to do is kneel and press your lips to their shoes in gratitude not because it happened but because it happened to them and knowing this you can go on believing it is somehow less likely to happen to you.

III

Poems from *At Once* (2004)

For the Morning

spiral of glory
poised on the vine,
I never tire

of your white trumpet
blazing flared edge
of color all

open to the oceanic
sort of end, thrashing red
snapper on the line,

an entire face falling
at the glacier's
distant crack.

Flower turning back
to the used-up
tissue, sticky

as the stillbirth?
Just as much work.
You don't know how much

you can really give.
You don't know how to live
but at once.

WHAT A HEART DOES BEST

Beneath tubes of trembling
yellow light a teacher warns
against lust and gluttony, the only
two deadly sins with any style.

She doesn't use those words exactly
but they know what she means
and I want to know where her high road leads
besides out of view of the glimmer

in this valley where a 6-year-old boy says:
when my heart hurts it feels like someone
punched me in the permanent teeth.
He says permanent

as in deadly, lasting or intending to last
like we intended those days to last
when the worst we knew
we would lose was teeth.

So lady you can leave me here,
knees bent and pressed against the cold
green linoleum of the past wishing
I again had fewer years than sins,

wishing all I knew about a heart is what
that boy's class does when I ask what theirs
know how to do. The whole room breaks
into a flapping, fingers folded as in church

and steeple. They thump the butts
of their palms like the pounding of two

bodies convincing two hearts all they have
lost is worth this coming together

and those children turn their faces up
insisting what a heart does best
is somehow keep itself beating *like this Miss.*
Mine goes like this.

After a God

The man I love most says one day
he will take a ballpoint pen and connect
the stars across this freckled
scoop of chest and milky way.
We'll cross the slope
of pale belly and name
the new constellation after a god
who shows people
all the places they might shine.

ADVICE

My father warned
　　　when in doubt

downshift.

Mom said *leave things*
better than you find them
especially bathrooms
　　　and hearts.

Grandmother Browne's tips for marriage
became the stuff of legend, a whisper
on her only daughter's wedding night.

Remember every age together
is the best age. Be hot in bed
and get yourself an egg pan.

Of course she denied it
until the very end
just like she denied being nearly two years older
than grandfather all sixty-one they were married.

He said *never write anything down*
that you wouldn't want
the whole world to read.

Before

the yellow pine floor was *done*
then mopped, carpets flopped,
warped windows
shaking as the spin cycle begins
there was another place
and footprints
       before boards Wind
before breathing
Leaves glittering in the back-light.

Out front a telephone pole leans
into lost voices.
They painted this porch ceiling
to look like sky
but now the pale
blue is peeling free.
The bees were never fooled.
Someone missed the corners
Left Cloud Left Cloud

FIELD TRIP

Three rows of wood ears pressed
to the chest of the dead cedar
while grimy vines still listen for breathing,
the silence of everything
turning back to dirt.

A small hand opens, offering
the dusky owl pellet, embedded
rat claws in gray fluff then points
to a blue ice cube tray sunk
by the bayou half full

of muddy water, full
of muddy sky.

I ask them to write
what they can't see, roots
of the Resurrection Fern clutching
up too high, the constant dying
of their own cell-splitting
bone skin minds.
But don't put that

Spanish Moss in your backpack
We can't see the new lives
waiting inside. I can't see

what might have been any different day deep
as the Congo of a child's asking.

Dark of heartness what
behind the blue? A full sky
behind the smallest eye?
What for the red water
winking back like a sign?

RECOGNIZABLE

I've been rumored to cut the blue
from bread and stare far
too long.

To make more than the occasional
Uppercase Mistake

and dig on through the backyard
garden full of red holes
       width of lost

seedlings all the while
knowing the blood-root of bamboo
is coming back.

Pulling it makes a fire
of my palms
       from the friction,
the question. Where is root? Stem?

Still asking the mud-caked mud-cracked.

Now remind me again
how I know you.

Acknowledgments

AGNI – "To the Man Who Stole the Trees We Planted in Memory of My Brother in Law Who Killed Himself Earlier in the Spring"

America Poetry Review – "Camping With Strangers"

Bat City Review – "The Multiple States of Matter"

Blackbird – "Boom"

Borderlands Texas Poetry Review – "Love Letter to a Stranger (Bird)" and "Love Letter to a Stranger (Dog)"

Cincinnati Review – "Not an Aubade"

ConnotationPress.com – "Melanoma"

Court Green – "The Cry Bone's Connected to the Why Bone." Reprinted in Verse Daily.

Forklift, Ohio – " The Season Of Mint"

Measure: An Annual Review of Formal Poetry – "Mexico"

Poet Lore – "Thoughts on the Past in Guadalupe County"

PoetryFoundation.org – "After a God"

Poets.org – "Love Letter to a Stranger (Stranger)"

Puerto Del Sol – "from The Presentation of Self in Everyday Life"

San Antonio Current – "What a Heart Does Best"

Southeast Review – "The Odds"

SWWIM.org – "Fellow Travelers"

The Awl – "Love Letter to a Stranger (China)"; "Love Letter to a Stranger (Kabul)"

The Hat – "Poetry"

The Nation – "Grey Wolf, Grizzly Bear, White-Tailed Deer"

Threepenny Review – "To Have Considered the Last of the Summer Mackerel"

Tin House – "Texas, Being"

"Love Letter to a Stranger" was included in *Poem-a-Day: 365 Poems for Every Occasion*. Harry Abrams, 2016.

"The Center for the Intrepid" was a winner in the 2010 Split This Rock Poetry Contest and published at www.splitthisrock.org.

"A Man Can Still Dream of Cigarettes" and "The Season When Some People Will Say." *Not for Mothers Only*. Albany, New York: Fence Books, SUNY, 2007, 380-381.

"Now, That is Summer" was included in the anthology: *Is This Forever or What: Poems from Texas.* Greenwillow/Harper Collins, 2005.

Poems from *At Once*, "The Second Reason" and "Dear Stranger" reprinted by Permission of University of Tampa Press.

ABOUT THE AUTHOR

A former James Michener Fellow at the University of Texas, Jenny Browne worked for many years as a poet in the schools through the Texas Commission on the Arts and is currently an associate professor of English and creative writing at Trinity University, where she teaches courses in creative writing, women and gender studies, and environmental literature. She has received the Cecil Hemley Memorial Award from the Poetry Society of America, a National Endowment for the Arts Fellowship in Poetry, and two creative writing fellowships from the Texas Writers League. Her poems and essays have appeared in numerous publications including *American Poetry Review, Boston Review, Garden and Gun, Oxford American, the New York Times,* and *Tin House*. Browne lives in downtown San Antonio, Texas, with her husband, photographer Scott Martin, and their daughters Lyda and Harriet.